Way *of* Wisdom

Way of Wisdom

Meditations on Love and Service

Emanuel Swedenborg

Edited by Grant R. Schnarr and Erik J. Buss

Chrysalis Books
West Chester, Pennsylvania

Library of Congress Cataloging-in-Publication Data

Swedenborg, Emanuel, 1688-1772.
Way of Wisdom: meditations on love and service / Emanuel Swedenborg;
edited by Grant R. Schnarr and Erik J. Buss.
p.   cm.
ISBN 0-87785-383-5
1. Swedenborg. Emanuel, 1688-1772—Quotations.   I. Schnarr, Grant R.
II. Buss, Erik J.   III. Title.
BX87711.A7S82   1999
289'.4—dc21   98-53150
CIP

Edited by Mary Lou Bertucci
Designed by Helene Krasney
Typeset in Berkeley by Helene Krasney Design
Printed in the United States of America

For more information on Chrysalis Books, contact: Swedenborg Foundation Publishers
320 North Church Street, West Chester, PA 19380 or http://www/swedenborg.com

For our wives, Cathy and Ann, companions on our way

Contents

Introduction

Even though truth is timeless, when it is understood by the mind and felt in the human heart, it makes all things new. The human spirit is lifted up to a new awareness of reality and of the spiritual possibilities in life.

Emanuel Swedenborg (1688–1772) wrote thirty volumes of theology and five volumes of his own spiritual experiences that set forth a new way of understanding God, heaven, and the self. It is a path to discovering a life of happiness and meaning—the way of wisdom.

Swedenborg's writings, which many believe to be divinely inspired, cover a variety of topics ranging from the nature of the Divine to surviving the depths of spiritual struggles.

Within the voluminous writings of Swedenborg are many precious gems of wisdom that stand alone—transcendent, beautiful, and relevant to an individual's spiritual quest. *The Way of Wisdom* is a collection of some gems mined from these works. In many cases these are not precise translations but have been restated in a modern idiom and put into a format similar to the popular wisdom books of the ages, introducing the spiritual seeker to what Swedenborg called "angelic wisdom." The passages were chosen to help with spiritual growth and understanding, to elicit deeper thought and meditation.

To allow the reader the opportunity for self-reflection and meditation, we have placed our own commentary on each passage at the back of the book. This commentary identifies the book from which the passage is derived.

This is not a book to be read through at one sitting. It has no plot, no characters, no narrative flow. Rather, it has moments of excitement—the rush of delight when the spirit apprehends truth. The passages are not arranged in a particular order; this has been done purposely to encourage the reader to let go of structure and to concentrate on each passage for the gem it is.

The aim of this little work is to bring insight and inspiration to the reader. We also hope this collection will motivate readers to delve more deeply into the works of Swedenborg, writings that contain treasures upon treasures of timeless wisdom.

Grant R. Schnarr and Erik J. Buss

Meditations

❧ 1 ❧

We are because God is.

 2

Because God is Love itself and Wisdom itself, God is Life itself.

 **3**

*All things are full of God, and all
take their portion from that fullness.*

4

*We cannot be spiritually reborn without some knowledge
of the new or spiritual life, of the true ideas that we ought
to believe and the good things that we ought to do. We cannot
learn these things on our own, because on our own
we can comprehend things only through our physical senses.
Our physical senses give us information about the material world
and ourselves, not about heaven and God. Spiritual knowledge
comes only from revelation.*

Only when we love God and show kindness toward our fellow human beings can we receive knowledge of the true way and have faith in it. We cannot do this when we live a life based on selfishness and materialism. If we lead a life of love and kindness, we are in the divine life. We can become joined to the divine life in no other way.

6

If people are earth-bound, they focus upon and love themselves and the material world. Spiritual people do not focus upon self and the material world, unless it serves to promote some spiritual service. Earth-bound people seem to themselves to have life when they are promoted to positions of importance and prestige over others. Spiritual people seem to themselves to have life in humility and in being the least. They do not ignore positions of importance, provided that these can be used to be of service to others.

*Earth-bound people experience bliss when they are richer
than others and possess the world's wealth. But when they become
spiritual, they are in their bliss when they have
knowledge of what is true and good,
which is their treasure.*

When we love our neighbors as ourselves, we do not perceive
delight in loving kindness except in its practice or in its use.
Therefore, a life of loving kindness is a life of useful service.
The life of heaven is like this. For the kingdom of God,
because it is a kingdom of mutual love,
is a kingdom of useful services. Every pleasure derived
from loving kindness has its delight
from its use or service.

To the extent that we detest evil, goodness enters from heaven.
To the extent that we detest promiscuity, what is chaste enters.
To the extent that we detest fraud and unlawful gains,
sincerity and justice enter.
To the extent that we detest hatred and revenge, loving kindness enters.
To the extent that we detest lies and blasphemies, truth enters.
And to the extent that we detest arrogance,
humility before God and love of others enter.

❧ 10 ❧

To shun evil is to do good.

*When you have a humble heart, you will know
that wisdom is perceiving that the things in which you
are wise are scarcely anything compared with the things
in which you are not wise.*

We cannot have humility when we love only ourselves.
Selfish love is hard, but love of the Divine is soft.

13

Selfish love must be completely crushed.

Heavenly love is loving what is good, honest, and just,
simply because it is good, honest and just,
and it is undertaking action from love.

 15

Heaven consists of a heartfelt desire
for the good of others rather than our own good.
It is serving others from love to promote their happiness,
not for the sake of any selfish hope of reward.

We cannot become angels, that is, come into heaven,
unless we bring something of an angelic character
from living in this world.
Present in this character is a knowledge
of the way from walking in it,
and a walking in the way through a knowledge of it.

❦ 17 ❦

Love and wisdom, without action,
are only imaginary concepts.
They become real when they are used.

*Thought from the eye closes the understanding,
but thought from the understanding opens the eye.*

*We attain enlightenment when we love truth
for the sake of truth, and not for the sake
of self-promotion or worldly gain.*

20

*Love consists in desiring to give what is one's own
to another. To feel the joy of another as joy
in oneself—that is loving.*

21

The Lord's church is spread over the whole globe, and so is universal. All who live a good life according to their own religious beliefs are members of it.

❧ 22 ❧

Heaven is of such a nature that all who have lived well,
of whatever religion, have a place there.

 **23**

Conscience is a new will and understanding implanted in us by God. So it is that God is present with us to the degree that we love goodness and truth.

*God's love goes forth not only to good people
but to evil people. God loves not only those who are
in heaven, but also those who choose hell,
for God is everywhere and forever the same.*

Two things make up the essence of God: Love and Wisdom.
The essence of God's Love is made up of three things:
to love others outside of himself, to desire to be one
with them, and to make them happy from himself.
These three also make the essence of God's Wisdom,
because Love and Wisdom are one in God.
Love desires these things and Wisdom puts them into effect.

26

All religion relates to life, and the life of religion is to do good.

 **27**

The life leading to heaven is not one withdrawn from the world, but a life active in the world.

28

A life of piety separated from a life of love
does not lead to heaven; only a life of love does.

29

As God's creation, we have been formed in such a way that
we can be more closely joined with him. We are joined not
by knowledge alone, or by intelligence alone, or even
by wisdom alone, but by living according to these.
The more closely we are joined with God,
the wiser and happier we become.

Every created thing is in itself inanimate and dead,
but it is animated and given life by this:
the Divine is in it, and it is in the Divine.

Every created thing is by nature a recipient of God.
It is able to be united with God because it was created
in God by God. And because it was created in this way, it is
an analogue and is like an image of God in a mirror.

In temptation we seem to be left to ourselves,
although this is not really the case, for God is then intimately
present in our inmost being and sustains us.
Therefore, when we overcome while in temptation,
we enter into a closer union with God.

The Lord does not withdraw us from our personal hell unless we see that we are in hell and wish to be led out.

 **34**

Innocence is the essential element
of love and goodness.

The heart of innocence is the acknowledgment
that all that is true and good comes from the Lord
and that none of it originates in oneself. And so,
innocence is a desire to be led by the Lord, not by self.

 **36**

Divine providence is universal.
It is present in the most minute things.

*Those who are in the stream of providence are
at all times carried along toward everything that is happy,
whatever may be the appearance of the means.
People who put their trust in God and attribute all things
to him are in the stream of providence.*

As far as we enter into the stream of providence,
we come into a state of peace.
As far as we are in a state of peace,
we are in divine providence.
Then we will know and believe that
the divine providence of God is in everything,
both in general and in particular.

 **39**

Nothing unconnected ever occurs,
for anything unconnected would instantly perish.

Hell and heaven are near to people, in fact, within people.
Hell exists within people who are in a state of evil.
Heaven exists within people who are in a state of goodness.
Even more than this, to the extent that people are receptive
of the goodness of heaven, they are in heaven right now.

After death everyone enters into the hell
or the heaven in which he or she had
predominantly chosen to live while in the world.

The Lord never judges anyone except from love, for he desires to raise all into heaven, and if it were possible, even to himself. For the Lord is Mercy and Goodness, and these cannot possibly condemn anyone.

43

If we choose to reject goodness, we condemn ourselves.

44

If in this earthly life we shunned goodness,
we will shun it in the afterlife, thus shunning the Lord;
for the Lord cannot be in anything except goodness.

❧ 45 ❧

All evil flows into us from hell, and all goodness flows into us through heaven from the Divine. But evil becomes a part of us when we believe and persuade ourselves that we think and do evil from our own being. In this way we make evil our own.

If we would believe what is really the case, then evil would not become part of us. For the moment that evil desire flows in, we would reflect that it comes from evil spirits; and as soon as we think this, the angels who are with us would ward it off and repel it.

 **46**

The truths we learn are like a mirror in which
we behold the face of God.

Prayer is truth coming from the heart,
and we are continually at prayer
when we live according to that truth.

*Genuine divine worship is unknown to those who
think worship exists only in reverence and prayers,
that is, from the mouth and thought alone, and
not in the work done from a good heart full of love and faith.
True worship of God consists in living according to God's ways.
This is also true love of God and true faith in God.
When we live a life of love and kindness,
our life is continual worship.*

 **49**

Love has power only through wisdom.

❧ **50** ❧

Faith is the eye of love.

 **51**

Evil has an appetite for falsity
and eagerly seizes upon it as if it were truth.

*If we wish to receive a heavenly selfhood, we must do
what is good and think what is true as if we were doing
and thinking by our own powers, but still believe that
all goodness and truth come from God.*

Whatever we love the most becomes our goal,
and we look toward it in everything we do.
It is present in our motivation like the imperceptible current
of a river that carries us along
even when we are thinking of other things,
for it is this that gives us life.

Love is the life of humanity.

 55

*It is a law of divine providence that we should not be
compelled by outward means to believe and love things that
belong to religion, but that we should bring ourselves
to believe and love, and sometimes compel ourselves.*

*When the body is no longer able to perform its functions
in the natural world, we are said to die. Yet we do not die,
but are only separated from the body that was useful in the world.
We still live; for we are not a person because of a body,
but because of spirit. It is the spirit in us that thinks,
and thought united to feelings is what makes a human being.
This life continues into the other; death is merely a transition.*

 57

We are not to blame for inborn tendencies toward evil
and will not suffer punishment in the other life because of them.
But we are punished for the evil that we have made our own
by how we lived our lives.

❧ 58 ❧

It is the universal order in the other life
that evil punishes itself, and so does falsehood.
Evil desires and false thoughts carry their own punishments
within them. And because there is such an order,
evil punishes itself, or, what is the same,
an evil person rushes into punishment,
answering to his or her evil.

Even the smallest moment of our lives involves a series of consequences extending to eternity. Each moment is like a new beginning to those that follow, and so with each and every one of the moments of our lives.

As one tone does not produce a harmony,
neither is a truth that stands alone complete.

The love in marriage of one man to one woman is the precious jewel of human life. This love produces states of innocence, peace, tranquility, inmost friendship, complete trust, and a mutual desire of the mind and heart to do everything good for each other. Because of these qualities, this love also produces bliss, rapture, delight, pleasure, and owing to an eternal enjoyment of states like these, the happiness of heaven.

*It is the nature of love to desire to share with another,
to give joy to another whom it loves from the heart,
and to seek its own joy in return from doing so.
Since this is the case, the divine love in the Lord
infinitely more wills to give joy to human beings,
whom he has created to receive both the love and wisdom
that radiate from him.*

63

Mercy is love that is grieving.

True wisdom is seeing what is beneficial to our eternal life and managing our present life according to that knowledge. We are truly wise when we not only know and grasp this with our understanding, but also will and do it.

Unless we do the good that we intend,
there is within us a failure to will that eventually
becomes lack of desire to act.

When we make truth the leader, goodness is obscure.
When we make goodness the leader, truth becomes visible
in its own light. To teach truth without goodness is to walk
as one who is blind, because goodness is what teaches and leads,
and truth is what is taught and led. Unless truth is illuminated
by goodness, or unless faith is enlightened by loving kindness,
there is nothing but darkness.

Truth does not shine from itself, because there is nothing flaming in it alone. It shines from goodness, for goodness is like a flame that gives forth light.

❦ 68 ❧

*We are not made happy by the true things we believe
from our faith, but by the goodness that comes from our faith.*

We cannot feel and perceive the divine life in the Word of God
except when we have a spiritual love for truth as we read it,
for then we are one with the Lord through the Word.
There is something intimately touching our hearts and spirits,
which flows with light into our understanding and bears witness.

Faith is truth acknowledged in the heart.

If you know all the good and truth that can be known,
but do not turn away from evil desires, you know nothing.
If you know from heaven all things that even angels ever know,
or if you know all things that are in revelation and in all the
teachings of our churches, and even all that the ancients have
written and councils decreed, and yet your will is evil, in the light
of heaven you will be looked upon as one who knows nothing,
because you do not will what you know.

It is utterly useless for you to know many things
if you do not live by what you know.
For knowledge has no other purpose than
that you may become spiritual through it.
When you have become spiritual, you have much more than
a person who knows countless things and yet is not spiritual.
For what the latter seeks by much knowledge, you already have.

What makes us human is not our form,
having a human face and a human body,
but having wisdom in our minds and goodness in our hearts.
We are truly human to the degree that we speak from sound reason
and look toward our home in heaven, while so far as we speak
from perverted logic and look toward our home in this world,
we move away from being truly human.

*Spiritual power is to desire the well-being of another
and to desire to give to another as far as possible
what is within us.*

To look upward to heaven is not merely to think about the things that belong to heaven, but to have these things as the goal and to love them more than all other things.

Since the angels in heaven receive goodness from the Lord,
they long for nothing more than to perform useful services.
These services are the very delight of their lives,
and it is from them that they enjoy bliss and happiness.

*You have achieved wisdom when you no longer have
any concern about understanding what is true and good,
but are willing and living it.*

The more nearly you become one with the Lord,
the more distinctly you appear to yourself
to be your own master,
and yet the more clearly you recognize
that you belong to the Lord.

In its essence, true love in marriage is nothing else than the willing of two to be one, that is, their desire that the two lives shall become one life.

So far as you approach and draw near to God,
doing so entirely as if of your own accord,
so far does God approach and draw near to you,
and becomes one with you in your inmost being.

We need to provide food and clothing for our bodies.
This is a first and primary goal.
But we do this so that we may have sound minds
in sound bodies. We need to provide food for the mind as well,
such things as relate to intelligence and wisdom,
so that our minds may be in a state to serve God.
If we do these things, we provide for our own good to eternity.
We must provide for ourselves, yet not for ourselves.

Spiritually focused people do not desire to retaliate,
doing evil in return for evil. They forgive from heavenly love.
They know that God protects all who are good from evil
and that he protects them according to the goodness in them.
Yet God cannot protect those who are inflamed with hostility,
hatred, and revenge, even when someone has wronged them,
because such people reject God's protection.

We are born without factual knowledge,
so that we may come into all knowledge
and progress into intelligence, and through this into wisdom.
We are born without love, so that we may come into all love.
By using what we have learned for love for God and others,
we become one with God, and by means of this
become truly human and enter into eternity.

84

We have a connection with the Divine,
and our inmost being is such that we can receive the Divine,
and not only receive it, but also make it our own
by acknowledgment and love, thus by reciprocating.
Since we are implanted in the Divine, we can never die.
For we are in what is eternal and infinite,
not only because it flows into us, but because we receive it.

*We become truly rational when our sensual life is ruled
by our spiritual life. But when our sensual life is not ruled
by the latter, we become sensual.
Whether we are rational or sensual can hardly be discerned
by others, but we can discern it if we explore our inner self,
the tendencies of our will and thought.*

86

We can receive some indication of whether we are rational or sensual from our own life— not as it appears, but from the inner quality that shows itself in our actions.

87

Our love for ourselves and our love
for the world are, by creation, heavenly loves.
They are loves of the natural part of us,
which serves spiritual loves as a foundation serves a house.
When we have no love of serving God and other people,
then, from being heavenly, those loves become hellish.

To prepare to receive and become one with God,
we must live within divine order.
The laws of order are all the commandments of God.

We can become one with God
only through love and loving actions,
love being the essence of spiritual connection.

Everything we confirm by our will and understanding remains
to eternity. What we confirm by our understanding alone
does not remain because what is of the understanding alone
is not within us but outside us, since it is only in our thoughts.
Nothing enters into and becomes part of us except what
is received by our will. This becomes part of our life's love.

 91

Evil loves cannot be removed from our minds
unless they appear. This does not mean that we should do evil
so that these desires may appear, but that we should examine
ourselves, not only our actions but also our thoughts,
and explore what we would do if we were not afraid
of laws and of losing our reputations.

*The Lord does not compel us to receive what flows in from himself,
but leads us while respecting our freedom. So far as we allow,
the Lord leads to what is good. So it is that the Lord leads us
through delights. He also leads through our illusions and resulting
false assumptions, gradually guiding us away from these.
It seems to us, however, as though we lead ourselves away.
The Lord does not shatter that assumption, for that would violate
our freedom, which must necessarily exist if we are to be reformed.*

If you wish to have perception in spiritual matters,
you must cultivate a love for truth grounded in goodness,
and must continually desire to know truth.
For then your mind will be illuminated.
When this happens, you can perceive something within yourself.
You do not have a love for truth if you receive all you know
from the doctrinal teachings of a church, simply because
a priest, an elder, or a leader has said that it is so.

❧ 94 ❧

The church of the Lord is not here or there, but everywhere,
even within those lands where the organized church does not dwell.
Wherever life is formed according to the principles
of loving kindness, we will find the church. Thus, the church
of the Lord is spread throughout the universal globe,
and yet is one. For when a life of loving kindness
makes up the church, and not doctrine separate from life,
then the church is one.

The evil acts that we consider allowable,
although we do not do them, become a part of us.
When we think any evil action allowable, we loosen its inward
restraint, and are kept from doing it only by outward restraints,
which are fears. And because our spirit approves such evil acts,
we do them freely when outward restraints are removed,
and in the meantime continually do them in our hearts.

We cannot have an exquisite perception of what is good,
or of what is blessed and happy, unless we have been
in the opposite state, in which we have experienced
what is not good, not blessed, and not happy.

We can be in doubt before we deny,
and we can be in doubt before we affirm.
When we doubt before we deny, we incline toward a life of evil.
When we doubt before we affirm, we incline to a life of goodness.
When negativity reigns in our hearts, our doubt cannot be removed,
for one misgiving avails more than a thousand confirmations.
One misgiving is like a grain of sand placed before the eye;
although it is single and small, it takes away all sight.

*It is no mark of intelligence
to be able to prove whatever one pleases.
But to be able to discern what is true as true
and what is false as false—
this is the mark and character of intelligence.*

Whatever spiritual quality we take on in the world remains after death. It is also increased and made more perfect to the extent that we love and desire goodness and truth, but not beyond it. For our character is measured by our desires.

*My friend, shun evil deeds and do what is good and
believe in the Lord with all your heart and all your soul,
and he will love you, and will give you a love
for doing what is good and the faith to believe.
Then from love you will do what is good,
and from faith, which is trust, you will believe.
If you persevere in doing this, a mutual union will occur
between you and God, which will be perpetual.
This union is what is meant by salvation and eternal life.*

Commentary

1   *Divine Providence ¶46*

Much of what is infinite cannot be comprehended by human beings because we are finite. However, when we raise our thoughts above thinking only in terms of time and space, a broader understanding of the infinite can be born. Humanity is connected to the infinite because humanity is created by and from the infinite. Humanity has reality because it is created by the source of reality. Swedenborg says, "Unless God were infinite, there would be no finite. Unless the infinite were the All there would be no reality; and unless God had created all things from himself there would be nothing. In a word, we are because God is."

2   *True Christian Religion ¶39*

All of creation is formed from the union of love and wisdom in God. This love and wisdom radiate forth as a sun from heaven, giving everything its heat and light, substance and form, motivation and understanding. All the love we feel is from the fire of God's love, and all the wisdom we acquire is from the light of that love from God. The union of love and wisdom is not only the source of life itself: it is life and is God.

3 *True Christian Religion ¶ 364*

Swedenborg writes, "The Lord flows into every human being with all his Divine love, and all his Divine wisdom, and so with all his Divine life." Genesis 2:7 speaks of this, where it says that Adam (who symbolizes humankind) was created an image of God, that God breathed into Adam's nostrils the breath of life, and that thus Adam became a living being. This is true not only in humans, but in all creation, for we are told, "The Lord is present everywhere, and where God is present, he is there with his whole essence."

4 *New Jerusalem and Its Heavenly Doctrine ¶ 177*

Spiritual rebirth takes place when we make spiritual values the focus of our lives. People who focus only on the material world can learn much about material things, but not much about spiritual things. The spiritual life can be lived in the material world and can even be confirmed in the vast panorama of God's creation, but the spiritual life comes from the spirit, not the flesh. In order to become wise, we must rise above the material world in search of truth and by means of revelation achieve wisdom. Revelation, the Word of God, raises human thought and fills it with knowledge of the way and of life. Revelation gives us an opportunity to rise above ourselves and the material world and to view life from heaven. It teaches God's point of view and how to live.

5   *Arcana Coelestia ¶2049 and 2588*

God cannot be found in selfish and material pursuits. In fact, the more we turn toward selfishness and material gain for fulfillment, the less fulfilled we become and the less able we are to see the true way to fulfillment. A way is opened to happiness and to heaven for those who strive to love God and their fellow human beings.

6 and 7   *Arcana Coelestia ¶3913*

In Matthew 6: 19–20, Jesus said, "Lay not up for yourselves treasure on earth, where moth and rust destroy, and where thieves break in and steal, but lay up for yourselves treasures in heaven, where neither moths nor rust destroy, and where thieves do not break in and steal, for where your treasure is, there your heart will be also." Swedenborg shows how this looks in our daily life. If we focus attention on selfishness and materialism, on promotion and earthly gain, we become earth-bound and not heaven-bound. Promotion and gain are not evil and can even be sought after, but the first priority for the heaven-bound is the spiritual richness of love for God and for fellow human beings, and of being of useful service to both. These are the treasures of heaven.

8   *Arcana Coelestia ¶997*

Love comes into being through useful service to others. In fact, the real joy of love is in its expression. Love that does not find expression soon dies.

9 and 10   *Apocalypse Explained ¶803*

People often ask what they should do to become good, spiritual beings. A better question to ask is, "What should I stop doing?" As far as we turn from evil, we turn toward the opposite good. This is the reason that most of the Ten

Commandments, the basic teachings of Judeo-Christian ethics, tell us what *not* to do.

11 *Apocalypse Explained* ¶828

Genuine wisdom involves humility. The wiser we become, the greater the realization that there is so much more to learn and understand.

12 and 13 *Spiritual Experiences* ¶4754

The opposite of humility is pride. Pride comes from an overruling love for self. As long as love for self rules, we cannot become humble. This limiting love must be, as Swedenborg says, completely crushed. However, to be "crushed" does not mean to be obliterated. The instinct for self-preservation and the desire to care for ourselves are God-given. They promote our welfare when they serve, but pervert us when they rule. To crush the love for self means to crush its desire to dominate and to subject it to higher loves: love for God and for our neighbor.

14 and 15   *Heaven and Hell ¶481 and 408*

Often people think of heaven as a place where people go to fulfill their dreams
and aspirations. This will truly be the case, if those dreams and aspirations are
derived from love and a desire to live a good life. Heavenly love is about serving others, and this love brings happiness like no other. In Matthew 20:27, Jesus
says, "Let whoever is chief among you be your servant." He showed us a
graphic example of this as recounted in John 13:3–17 by washing his disciples' s
feet—a duty that the lowest servants performed—to show that even he was not
above desiring to serve. The greatest in the kingdom of heaven are those who
have the greatest desire to be of service from love.

16   *Divine Providence ¶60*

We were born to become angels. Life in this world is a preparation period for
an eternity to come. In *Divine Providence,* paragraph 277a, Swedenborg says
"Where the tree falls there it lies. So also does a person's life when he dies remain
such as it has been." We can continue perfecting areas we have actively worked

on in this life, but this will not result in a different angelic character, just a better version of the same one.

17   *Apocalypse Revealed ¶875*

What is love without the understanding of how to express it, or wisdom without love to guide and motivate it? They are nothing. What are love and wisdom without action, or a life where these can find fulfillment? They are nothing. Love and wisdom are only actual, that is, *real,* if they are used in life.

18 and 19   *Divine Love and Wisdom ¶46*
                                        Arcana Coelestia ¶9424

If we look at the world with natural eyes alone, that is, from a materialistic view-point, only the natural, material world will be seen. Focusing on the earth alone closes spiritual sight. How can we look up if looking down? How can we look within if looking without? But when we shift our focus to what is spiritual, searching for ultimate truth behind the veils of the way things appear, we find true understanding of life on all levels. This is what Jesus meant on a deeper level when he said in Matthew 6:33, "Seek first the kingdom of God and his righteousness, and all these things will be added to you."

20 *Divine Love and Wisdom* ¶47

The context of this passage speaks of God's love for the human race and how God created human beings to be receiving vessels of his love. Love has within it a desire for oneness, or conjunction. It must be mutual in order to be true love. Therefore, in its full text, Swedenborg's ideas focus on the responsiveness of love: "It is an essential quality of love not to love self, but to love others, and to be joined with others by love. It is also an essential quality of love to be loved by others, for this is how the conjunction takes place. The essence of all love lies in conjunction. This, in fact, is its life, which is called enjoyment, pleasantness, delight, sweetness, bliss, happiness, and felicity. Love consists in this, that its own should be another's. To feel the joy of another as joy in oneself, that is loving. But to feel one's own joy in another and not the other's joy in oneself is not loving. This is loving self, while the former love is loving the neighbor."

21 and 22

Heaven and Hell ¶328
Divine Providence ¶330

The idea that anyone must confess faith in a certain name of God or belong to a specific church organization to enter heaven is a hurtful and untrue message. God is a God of love. Though people of different religions may call him different names, he is the same God who is worshiped. God does not judge people according to what religion they may have grown up with or adopted. Instead, he looks at the heart. The message is very simple, comforting, and logical: heaven is made up of good people, because good people have heaven within themselves, regardless of their religious beliefs.

23

Arcana Coelestia ¶4299

To leave human beings in the greatest possible freedom, the Divine becomes present with us only as far as we choose to welcome that presence. A home is created in which God can dwell by the birth of a new will, or desire for good and a new and growing understanding of truth. Therefore, the Lord says in Revelation 3:20, "Behold I stand at the door and knock. If anyone hears my voice and opens the door, I will come into him, and dine with him, and he with me."

24   *True Christian Religion ¶43*

It may be a surprise to learn that God loves people in a state of evil as well as those in a state of goodness, that he loves those in hell as well as those in heaven. But could a God who truly is a God of pure love and mercy feel any differently? God doesn't reject people; people reject God. Heaven is for those who receive God's love and wisdom and integrate those qualities into their own lives. Hell is for those who freely choose a life apart from that love. God still loves those in hell, but they do not accept that love or use it in their lives.

25   *True Christian Religion ¶43*

Love needs to focus on others apart from self. We can even think of loving others as loving in others whatever is different from what is in us. Loving what is like ourselves in others is simply loving ourselves in them. Within that love is the desire to become one with the person and to bless the person with happiness. That is why God created every human being: to love each person as a unique individual, to become one with each, and to bless each with happiness.

26   *Doctrine of Life ¶1*

Religious philosophy or doctrine is meaningful only insofar as it leads a person to improve his or her life. In fact, unless any teaching or precept leads to living a good life, it is not from God.

27 and 28   *Heaven and Hell ¶535*

There are times when a retreat from day-to-day responsibilities and interaction with society may be beneficial for renewal. But the spiritual way is not achieved by becoming a hermit. A spiritual path can be followed only through a useful life, interacting and growing with people. A life apart from society and useful service to society limits the challenges and the opportunities for growth. We cannot love the neighbor if there is no neighbor to be loved. We cannot practice loving kindness through useful service if no service is performed. A spiritual life is not lived apart from the world, but in and within the world.

2 9 *Divine Providence ¶32, 33, and 37*

Thought or understanding about God does bring us closer to God. But living a good life conjoins us to God and is the way to ever-increasing happiness.

3 0 *Divine Love and Wisdom ¶53*

Swedenborg asserts that the world of nature is not divine. Creation apart from God is dead. But the Divine flows into all creation and not only gives it life, but is reflected in it.

3 1 *Divine Love and Wisdom ¶56*

The ancients learned much about God and spirituality through nature. It was their Bible, so to speak. However, through the process of time, people began to focus more on the material aspects of nature rather than the spiritual life that is reflected within it. People ceased to see the reflection of God in nature and so lost a connection with him. This connection can be reestablished, and the Creator can be seen once again, through all of creation.

3 2   *True Christian Religion ¶126*

Temptation is a struggle between opposing values within each of us. It is a battle between good and evil for dominion. In the heat of this battle, it may seem that we struggle alone, but we are not alone. The reality is that God is actually more present and active in times of temptation than at other times because the stakes are higher. God allows us to feel alone during temptations so that we may freely choose, without any coercion, whether good or evil will rule. Once a choice for good is made, the divine presence can manifest itself, because it has been freely invited to do so.

3 3   *Divine Providence ¶251*

Heaven and hell are actual spiritual abodes, but they are also states of life and of mind. We create our own heaven and hell by the free choices we make in life.

For those of us who are trying to escape the hell we have created for ourselves, the Lord is always ready to offer a hand and draw us up to higher ground. But this cannot be accomplished unless we see the state we are in, desire to be set free, and take his hand.

34 and 35 *Arcana Coelestia ¶3994 and 10210*

The innocence of a child is a beautiful thing, but it is an innocence stemming from ignorance. The innocence that accompanies the spiritual life is a wise innocence. It is knowing that there are ways contrary to God's will, but nevertheless having a willingness to be led by the Divine.

36, 37, and 38 *Arcana Coelestia ¶8478*

There are many currents in people's lives. One current is stronger and at the same time gentler than the rest, though this may seem like a paradox. It is the stream of God's providence. Sometimes the quest for the spiritual life isn't so much a matter of a tenacious search or struggle to change, but rather a letting go. Simply acknowledging and accepting that God is leading and that we are following can change us. When we drift into this steady stream of God's guidance, it leads to all good things.

39 *Arcana Coelestia ¶2556*

There is no such thing as a vacuum. All things are connected in spirit.

40 and 41 *Arcana Coelestia ¶8918*
Heaven and Hell ¶203

Our spirits are a microcosm of our greater connection with either heaven or hell. Heaven and hell are not only places we go to after death, but are also states that exist within our spirit right now.

42, 43, and 44 *Arcana Coelestia ¶2335*

This is a new concept: God doesn't punish us. We punish ourselves because evil and disorder bring their own punishments. If God truly is a God of love, he would not and could not condemn people to an eternity of misery. But God does allow us to reject him, his love, compassion, and the happiness that comes from him. This concept presents a God who is truly and fully a God of love who, at the same time, respects our freedom and individuality.

45 *Arcana Coelestia ¶6206*

In Matthew 15:11, Jesus says, "It is not what goes into the mouth that defiles a man, but what comes out of the mouth that defiles a man." All our inclinations to think or do what is good or evil come from the spiritual world, from the angels and evil spirits present with us. A person is not to blame for the evil thoughts that spring up, seemingly from nowhere. Nor should anyone take credit for being the origin of the good and true things that enter the mind, as if out of the blue. Neither good nor evil originates in us. But we make those thoughts and inclinations our own by holding them in our minds and hearts, and by acting upon them. Swedenborg asserts that keeping aware of this spiritual reality gives us a powerful tool for regulating our inner lives. With this awareness, evil is easily rejected, and goodness is incorporated into life with humility and gratitude.

46   *True Christian Religion ¶6*

Every true idea is imprinted with the face of God.

47   *Apocalypse Explained ¶493*

When we pray from the heart, there comes an answer in the form of a gentle perception of some truth. When we live by that truth, our lives become a living prayer.

48   *Arcana Coelestia ¶10143 and 1618*

Following the last passage, genuine worship is part of life. We ultimately worship God by living God's will. A life in God and from God exceeds any prayer from the lips or even feelings of reverence from the heart, because this life is one with God.

49 and 50   *True Christian Religion ¶784*
                                        Arcana Coelestia ¶ 3863

Some poets have asserted that love is blind. But spiritual love is far from blind;

rather, it is illuminated by wisdom. Love desires to see and to know how to go forward into life. The faith that comes with religion gives that love sight, direction, focus, and power.

51 *Arcana Coelestia ¶10648*

When we have a desire to do something wrong, we usually find a way of justifying it. This is the desire of evil to find some falsehood to mask its intent and create an excuse to go forward into disorder.

52 *Arcana Coelestia ¶2883*

The Christian religion has made much of the fact that a person can do nothing that is truly good apart from God. Some have used this to justify the idea that people are saved by their faith alone, apart from any personal action. Swedenborg asserts that, while it is true that human beings can do no good apart from God, they must act *as if* by themselves in living a good life, in order to find salvation. In other words, faith must be expressed in action or it is not true faith. But when faith does turn into action, it is not the person alone who lives a life of goodness, but God in the person. When Peter had enough faith to walk on the turbulent sea toward his Savior, it was God who kept him afloat, but he still had to walk.

53   *New Jerusalem and Its Heavenly Doctrine ¶56*
Each of us has a ruling motivation or love that guides us along in life. This love can change and grow into what is heavenly or hellish. It is the core of who we are as human beings and the current within which we navigate our lives. We make many mistakes on our journey, but if our central love is heavenly, we embrace God's love in our souls.

54   *Divine Love and Wisdom ¶1*
Swedenborg wrote, "People know that there is such a thing as love, but they do not know what love is. . . . And because people are unable, when they reflect upon it, to form any idea or thought about love, they say either that it is nothing, or that it is merely something flowing from the sight, hearing, touch, or communication with others, and thus affecting them. They are completely

unaware that love is their very life. It is not only the general life of the whole body, and the general life of all thoughts, but also the life of all their particular loves and thoughts. . . . Love is the life of humanity."

55   *Divine Providence ¶129*

There is nothing more important to most people than their own freedom, especially freedom to think, feel, and live the way they choose. Forcing people to believe certain religious principles takes away that freedom and actually closes the mind to deeper insight. Freedom and spirituality go hand in hand; remove the one, and you remove the other. However, a person may find it necessary to compel him- or herself to live the spiritual life, choosing, for instance, to resist evil thoughts or actions and to pursue peace and goodness. This is the way to spiritual growth because self-compulsion is a free act leading to goodness.

Life in this world is a preparation for an eternity to come. The body is only a temporary home for the spirit within. When the body is no longer able to house our spirits, we are freed from earthly life and awaken to a very real world, a world for which we were born. Those who have begun that inner growth while in the world continue to grow in so many different ways while in heaven in love, wisdom, beauty, connection with God and fellow human beings, in happiness, and even joy. They become angels.

God does not judge and condemn a person for what he or she may be inclined to do. "There is nothing that enters a person from outside which can defile him; but the things which come out of him, those are the things that defile a person," we are told in Matthew 7:15. In fact, God does not ever judge or condemn a person because of any evil, in inclination or actuality. Evil judges itself and brings its own punishment. When we are tempted to act on destructive inclinations, we have a choice. We can, with God's help, choose not to act on these inclinations. But when we freely choose to love, act, and take pleasure in destructive ways, the evil becomes a part of our very nature, and brings its own misery and its own punishment. In the final analysis, people are not actually sent to hell or heaven, but create a hell or heaven for themselves.

59

Arcana Coelestia ¶4690

Take a pebble and drop it into a still pool of water. You can see the circular ripple expand outward indefinitely from that first point. This is a representation of a life's effect on the world, and, in fact, on the universe. This is also a representation of every action's effect on the universe. Ripple after ripple, the moments of our lives send forth their energy and effect into the universe, causing a change, making a difference. Knowing this brings new incentive to live a loving, productive life.

One true idea standing alone is easily denied or twisted to sound like something else. Two or more true ideas confirm in our minds the authenticity of the idea itself. One true idea can act as a witness to the other, and vice versa. In fact, they harmonize with each other and help to perfect each other. It is music to our inner hearing.

The love of a woman and a man is precious because it embodies the union of love and wisdom in God and also in all creation. Wisdom and love desire to be one and have no greater delight than when they are one. This oneness is reflected, embodied, and lived in the marriage of one man and one woman. Swedenborg says, "Love in marriage is the precious jewel of human life because a person's life is just like the love in him. That love makes the inmost element of his life, for it is the life of wisdom dwelling together with its love, and of love dwelling together with its wisdom, and so it is the life of the delights of both. In a word, a person is a living soul as a result of that love."

63   *Arcana Coelestia ¶5480*

God's love for the human race is all encompassing. The Divine is not distant, indifferent, detached. God is human, a Divine Human, and even as his love rejoices in our own joy, his mercy grieves with us in our times of grief and pain. We are never alone.

64   *Apocalypse Explained ¶338*

Modern life places too much emphasis on the here and now. Though it is important not to focus full attention on a particular time in the distant future, raising our thoughts above time and space toward what is infinite and eternal raises our mind above the whirlwind of temporal life. When we look to eternal life and the eternal consequences of our actions, we live not only on a horizontal plane of material thoughts, feelings, and concerns, but on a vertical plane, connected to the infinite. This produces thoughts, feelings, and concerns of a spiritual nature. This is wisdom, because looking to what is eternal connects us to God.

65   *Divine Providence ¶151*

There is an old familiar saying, "The road to hell is paved with good intentions." This is because to intend a good deed but never to act upon it is actually a failure of goodwill. Swedenborg takes this a step further by asserting that, when we fail to act on our good intentions, we lose the intention itself. Love needs a home in action or it will die.

66 and 67   *Arcana Coelestia ¶2407, 4844, and 4742*

A person can say something "truthful" that is literally correct but not necessarily right. Similarly, a person can express something true that isn't necessarily good. To speak the truth alone without love is to speak from judgment without mercy. Love gives truth its light and its healing power. Any real truth has love within it and leads to good actions.

68 *Arcana Coelestia ¶4984*

If we know the truth, the truth will, indeed, make us free. But if we know and live by what is good, we will find happiness.

69 *Apocalyplse Revealed ¶200*

Swedenborg says that the Bible, or the Word of God, is a special book. It contains deeper and deeper symbolic meanings. Because of this, the wisdom of God rests within every saying, story, and image presented in Scripture. The literal meaning acts as a body, housing the soul of God's wisdom within. But this deeper wisdom is not apparent to the casual observer. It becomes apparent to those who approach the Word of God with a humble heart to learn about God, about life, and about self-improvement. For these, the Word of God becomes an unending and ever-increasing source of not only wisdom, but of communication with the Divine. This is why it is called the Word of God.

70 *Apocalypse Explained ¶813*

Faith is not blind, as some would say. Faith is seeing the truth and having confidence in it. Real faith is not just a matter of the mind, but of the heart as well.

71
Apocalypse Explained ¶1180
De Verbo ¶29

To flee from evil thoughts and deeds is the beginning of wisdom and spiritual life. Evil blocks love, while denial and false thinking block true wisdom. The greatest priority in spiritual growth is to discover the most dangerous selfish desire in our life, to ask God to remove it, and then to act in cooperation with God to begin a new life without it.

72
Arcana Coelestia ¶1100

Sometimes we think that if we only read enough books about a certain challenge we are facing, or if we can get the right insight, we will find the answers we need and be cured. But this is not the case. Religious people often fall into the trap of thinking they will be happy and find salvation by their belief alone apart from how they live their lives, and they sometimes even believe they are better than others because they belong to the "right" faith. But belief is useless if it is not practiced in life, even as knowledge is useless unless it is put into practice. Knowledge or faith does not produce happiness in the believer. Rather, the goodness that comes from a life of faith accomplishes this.

73   *True Christian Religion ¶417*

Humans, unlike animals, can rise above their nature. A lion, for instance, cannot say, "I think I'll stop killing and become a vegetarian." A human can rise above base wants and desires, and change to something more noble and more spiritual than what he or she started out to be. This ability makes us human. In fact, since we are created in God's image, the more noble and spiritual we become, the more human we become, because we come into a greater likeness of God, who is the Divine Human.

74   *Apocalypse Explained ¶79*

We might think of power as the ability to move people or objects in the direction of our choosing. But this is not true spiritual power, the kind that brings happiness, healing, and life. Real power is from God. The power of life itself and all its healing qualities come from love. To desire to give to others from our very being makes us powerful because this desire contains the creative force of God's love within it.

75 *Arcana Coelestia ¶7693*

Some people think of heaven as a place they will go some day if they are good enough or lucky enough to be let in. Swedenborg reiterates Jesus' own words that the kingdom of God is within us. To look to heaven is to look to what is good right now in our lives and to have a good and loving life as our daily goal. When we love what is good and right, we love heaven itself. Living by these noble goals, we become heavenly. And having become heavenly, we enter this realm when we shed our earthly bodies at the time of death.

76 *Arcana Coelestia ¶6073*

We have heard the expression, "Idleness is the devil's pillow." On the other hand, useful service is the angels' playground. Swedenborg says that the kingdom of heaven is a kingdom of useful service, where angels help and support one another (as well as people on earth) in a loving community. Being useful brings happiness, whereas idleness often brings depression and sorrow. Spiritually, we get what we give.

77 *Arcana Coelestia ¶10225*

Wisdom is a quality of the heart and of life. When we attain wisdom, the issue is no longer a struggle to understand what is good and true, because what is good and true has become so incorporated into daily life that we become an embodiment of those values and loves.

78 *Divine Providence ¶42*

This is one of the paradoxes of spiritual growth. The more we surrender to the divine will and acknowledge that all life is from the Divine, the more we feel life to be our own and the more freedom we will enjoy. This is because a life based on loving kindness and doing God's will is freedom itself. It is liberating and enlivening, and carries a blessing far beyond any other way of life.

79 *Conjugial Love ¶215*

God is waiting to give us many gifts as we become willing and able to receive them. One of the most precious gifts is a soulmate, the other half of a person. As two married people grow spiritually—shunning lustful thoughts and desires as offensive and making efforts to love and be considerate of each other—God endows them with a growing desire to become one human being. Each person maintains his or her individuality, at the same time that the couple experiences a joy and oneness unknown before this. This joy increases to eternity as they take each small step forward toward oneness day by day.

80 *True Christian Religion ¶89*

When we do anything good, it feels like that effort comes from self. And it feels to us as if we accomplish a spiritual goal alone. The reality is that God is present, unseen, doing the real work. We make a small effort in the outward world, and God enters into our souls and brings union, and so creates new life in our spirits.

81 *Arcana Coelestia ¶ 6936 and 6937*

Some people think that we need to deny all personal needs to become spiritual, renouncing worldly pleasure and gain, even hating self. God wants us to take care of ourselves, provide for ourselves, and love ourselves. In fact, he knows that we need to do this first, before trying to take care of others. But the motivation is crucial. The purpose of taking care of ourselves first is to be able to serve others better.

82 *Apocalypse Explained ¶ 556*

"To err is human; to forgive Divine," Alexander Pope wrote. Swedenborg teaches that the capacity to forgive comes from the divine presence within us. As we grow spiritually, we gain a growing sense of God's protection, which imbues us with an inner sense of safety.

Lao Tzu says, "If you want to become full, let yourself be empty." In relation to this, Swedenborg, along with John Locke, says that people are born empty, so that they can become filled. In fact, the emptiness itself serves a spiritual purpose. Because we have no built-in spiritual character, we can choose completely what kind of spiritual character we will have. We choose to become truly human by receiving the love and wisdom from God that elevates our actions from natural to spiritual.

Each person is connected to an infinite source of love, life, and wisdom. It can seem hard to conceive of living forever, or of overcoming the challenges that we sometimes face. And by ourselves, it would be impossible. But because our innermost beings are linked to a divine being, we can tap into infinite power, infinite love, and infinite perspective. The more we receive that life, the more alive we feel.

85 and 86

Swedenborg uses the term "rational" to mean the part of us that can lift itself above daily experience to put things into perspective and to make comparisons and see contrasts. These passages describe a tension we all experience: to live either from what our senses tell us or to lift our minds up and choose a higher path. It is very hard to see whether someone else is being rational or sensual, but we can look at our own lives and see the reasons we are motivated to act as we do. We can also receive hints as to the motivations of others by observing their lives, although we will never be certain.

87
Divine Love and Wisdom ¶396

Loving self and the pleasures the world has to offer is good. God wants us all to enjoy pleasure and to have healthy self-esteem. These qualities are foundational to everyone's spiritual well-being. But unless we love God and each other at the same time, loving self becomes egocentricity and loving what the world has to offer becomes materialism.

88 and 89

True Christian Religion ¶396
Arcana Coelestia ¶2349

Some people try to receive God by obeying all the rules, but they neglect to act in loving ways. Others feel that, if they are loving, they will be connected to God, but they do not stop to think about how to be truly loving. True spirituality is a balance of love and wisdom, of mercy and order, of thought and action. The main way of becoming loving is to submit to the laws of order, to follow God's path.

90

Divine Providence ¶318

We all know far more true things than we apply to our lives. Those truths we know but do not enact in our lives are like dusty books on a shelf; they serve no purpose. Living a true idea internalizes it. After a time, that truth becomes written on our hearts, as God says of his people: "I will put my law in their minds, and write it on their hearts; and I will be their God" (Jeremiah 31:33).

91

Divine Providence ¶ 278

If a dangerous disease is discovered early enough, a person can often recover fully. We achieve spiritual health when we examine our hearts, minds, and lives to see if secret desires are causing spiritual harm. The best way to discover these inner thoughts is to ask ourselves what we would do if there were no consequences. In other words, what evil actions do we refrain from simply because of external consequences like punishments or damage to reputation? Regular self-examination brings these desires to light so we can deal with them before they cause harm.

92 *Arcana Coelestia ¶6472*

In some ways, God can be viewed as a pragmatist. God sees what we know and believe, and works with whatever is available to help us move forward spiritually. Sometimes he will work with our illusions about what is true, sometimes with genuine truths. At each step, however, the Lord absolutely respects our freedom, never forcing, always appealing to what is delightful.

93 *Arcana Coelestia ¶5937*

We learn facts about spiritual life from external sources, such as revelation, spiritual authorities, or a church. That knowledge in itself does not give us a perception about spiritual matters. To achieve that perception, we need to develop a love for truth for the sake of the goodness that the truth leads to. When we approach life from this perspective, God grants an inner perception of the truth within those facts and a wisdom about how to apply them.

94 *Arcana Coelestia ¶8152*

The Lord's church on earth is not a body of people who gather in church buildings once a week. It is a spiritual entity made up of all who sincerely live according to the principles of love that they understand, whether they attend church or not. "The kingdom of God does not come with observation; nor will they say, 'See here!' or 'See there!' For indeed, the kingdom of God is within you," Jesus tells us in Luke 17:20-21. When people view each other from the perspective of the life they lead, rather than the doctrine they espouse, they can feel a kinship with all good people around the world. This is God's spiritual church.

95   *Divine Providence ¶81*

In Matthew 5:27–28, Jesus tells us, "You have heard that it was said to those of old, 'You shall not commit adultery.' But I say to you that whoever looks at a woman to lust for her has already committed adultery with her in his heart." Jesus on earth raises the standard for what constitutes the spiritual life. It is not good enough just to restrain from externally committing a sin, while actively fantasizing about it. A great deal can be learned by examining our fantasy life.

96   *Arcana Coelestia ¶2694*

Any person on a spiritual journey experiences times of elation and times of pain and darkness. We need both because we learn by contrasts. In *Heaven and Hell*, paragraph 158, Swedenborg writes about the ups and downs even angels experience: "I have been taught from heaven why there are such changes of state there. The angels said that there are many reasons. The first is that the delight of life and of heaven . . . would gradually lose its value if they experienced it continually, just as happens with people who experience pleasures and comforts without variety.

A second reason is that angels have a sense of self apart from God, just as people on earth do. It is loving self, and all in heaven are withheld from this sense of self apart from God. To the extent that they are kept away from it by the Lord, they receive love and wisdom. But to the extent that they are not kept away, they experience selfish love.. . . . A third reason is that fluctuation of state helps perfect them, because they become used to being held in love for the Lord and withheld from selfish love. By fluctuations between delightful experiences and undelightful experiences, their perception and awareness of goodness becomes more exquisite."

97   *Arcana Coelestia ¶2568 and 6479*

Is the glass half full or half empty? Do you look at an idea seeking to affirm the truth that is in it, or seek to cut down and deny? In our sight of truth, attitude is everything.

98   *True Christian Religion ¶334*

Intelligence is not about our being powerful and capable. True intelligence is about learning to submit our mind to the truth, to perceive it as something greater than ourselves, rather than to twist and manipulate it.

Because we are finite, we can continue to be perfected for eternity. We each choose what our spiritual character will be in this world. Then, after death, we continue to refine and perfect what we have chosen to value above all else. Everyone has limits, but only those that are self-imposed restrict our desire to progress spiritually. The infinite, divine life is available to everyone, giving us whatever we need and want.

Spiritual life is sometimes portrayed as a hard journey involving pain and suffering. It does not have to be. The spiritual path involves two essential steps: believing in a Being greater than self (God) and living according to whatever principles of truth you believe. Following these simple steps starts us on the path. Once we are on the path, God can guide our steps; he will give us an inner love for the Divine and the strength to follow the path.

Emanuel Swedenborg
(1 6 8 8 — 1 7 7 2)

Emanuel Swedenborg's many books offer a theology that is respectful and inclusive of other religions, yet presents many unique insights and perspectives on the Bible, God, and our lives.

Swedenborg, the son of a Lutheran bishop, began his career as a scientist. Later in life, his interests began to turn toward more philosophical matters, specifically to finding the seat of the soul in the body. This changing focus from science to philosophy progressed to an interest in theology. Swedenborg reported that he gradually began to have spiritual experiences during the early 1740s and that, for the last twenty-seven years of his life, he entered the spiritual world and talked with angels and devils.

Swedenborg wrote thirty volumes of theology and five volumes of his personal experiences, entitled *Spiritual Experiences*. He did not try to found a church himself nor did he ever seek any accolades or honors for his work. He did, however, believe that a church would arise based on revelations from God and on the Bible. He considered his works to be a divine revelation that would usher in a new spiritual era involving a return to the true focus of Christianity. That focus is that Jesus Christ is God, the manifestation of the invisible Divine just as our minds and bodies are the manifestations of our invisible soul, and that heaven is achieved by living a good life based on what we know and understand, not on faith alone.

Swedenborg taught that there is an inner meaning to the Bible, that the Word is the vehicle for a deeper meaning that describes the individual's spiritual struggles. Each battle, law, or healing in Scripture describes an inner battle people face, a law of spiritual reality, or a way that the spirit can receive healing. Over half of his theological writings, works such as *Arcana Coelestia, Apocalypse Explained,* and *Apocalypse Revealed,* focuses on presenting a symbolic understanding of the Bible.

Most of Swedenborg's work revolves around themes of becoming a more spiritual person. The basic principles are simple, but he offers a great deal of other information to aid people in their journey. He provides steps to overcome spiritual dysfunction that are remarkably similar to modern day twelve-step programs.

Swedenborg also wrote a great deal about the nature of God and his providence. He posits that God is a being of pure love and pure wisdom, infinite and eternal, but also human. Humankind is created in the image of God, so what we think of as loving is an image of God's infinite love. The one God took on a human body in the form of Jesus Christ. By his life on earth, he purified that body and human mind of all finite limitations until it became a perfect vessel of the divine soul within it. Thus, Jesus Christ is the embodiment of the one God, the mind and body of the infinite soul of God.

Swedenborg's heaven is more real and varied than any other description of that fabled realm. In his best-known work, *Heaven and Hell,* he describes a place that is vital and active, much like this world, where people have homes, jobs (which they love to do because those roles are an expression of their deepest desire to serve), social life, marriages, books, and more. Heaven is heaven because of the like-minded people there, and hell is hell for the same reason. We literally create our own heaven or hell.

Swedenborg wrote about much more, most notably a new way of understanding the teachings about the Last Judgment portrayed in Revelation, the true nature of married love, and the nature of creation. His writings reveal a new path to spiritual discovery and to living a life that brings rewards here and in the hereafter.